What
The FOUR Core Networking Types

MW01519933

Carol's book not only gives us important tools for effectively communicating with potential business partners and customers, but also for honoring our differences and bringing out the best in our team members. Every serious network marketer will want to know and teach how to apply the FOUR Core Networking Types.

Marian Head
Author, *Revolutionary Agreements*

If you are looking for a way to get on the fast track to business success, The FOUR Core Networking Types is a must read. Applying the skills in this book will have a significant impact on every one of your business and personal relationships.

Terry Petrovick
Million Dollar Income Earner

I thoroughly enjoyed reading The FOUR Core Networking Types. Not only did I gain insight as to how my own personality operates, I learned more about how to prospect AND support other personality types. This book makes a valuable addition to any networker's library.

Connie Godenick, M.D.
Network Marketing Professional

You may have attended workshops, listened to numerous audios, or read various books on this topic. The FOUR Core Networking Types puts it all together in one place, with practical comparison charts, and insights to help anyone build a successful team."

David Rundle
Top Producer, Ontario Canada

The Four Core Networking Types is a simple, yet effective tool for helping us communicate with not only new prospects, but other leaders as well.

Poni Altvater
Million Dollar Income Earner

To understand people is foundational in building a healthy and effective network. The FOUR Core Networking Types gives you insight into people's strengths and teaches you how to best connect with others. Often, the only reason we lack success in network marketing is simply because we don't understand people, including ourselves! Enjoy The FOUR Core Networking Types. Success is just an insight away.

Cheryl Townsley N.D.

In the business of networking, it's imperative that you communicate well. Knowing both your personality and that of those you are speaking to, facilitates communication that is more successful. This book accomplishes that goal.

Ray Robbins
Multi Million Dollar Income Earner

Praise for the Four Core Networking Types Workshop

This was the single most effective training I have taken yet, since joining my company. I finally feel like I have some useful information that I can use in not only business but in my every day life on how to t talk to people the way they need to hear and learn, because it is not about me! I can apply this in my life every day.
Linda Sztanko
Welland, ON

Thank you for researching and teaching us a vital aspect to not only being successful but to "love with power" through understanding personality types. You empowered me to transform my thinking to have confidence in my personality quadrant. I enjoyed how to discover what quadrant of personality I am to be more effective and to appreciate and love who I am instead of using that velvet hammer.
Satu Tanninen
Burlington, ON

This type of workshop is an eye opener as to the individual personalities and how one can benefit in every aspect of life, work, family, etc. I loved the hands on and the role playing.
Helga Altmann
Innisfil, ON

This workshop truly opened my eyes to see that different people respond and react very differently to each other. I know now that I need to change my approach when speaking to various personality types. Thank you so much! I loved the public introspection in a safe setting.
Juergen Harder
St, Catherines, ON

This workshop was a great eye opening about what I am doing and what I need to change to increase my business and learning how to work with my wife as she is a Professor and I am an Entertainer. I loved getting to know myself.
Paul Mann
London, ON.

Excellent training for business and life. I have learned to important it is to be aware of others and how to respond to them in a way that they feel important. I had some good laughs. Now I see how different personalities can work together as a team.
Jane Adamson
Burlington, ON

This workshop had great information and practical tools for improving my people skills that can be use with my business, my family, and my friends. I enjoyed the good information and slides. Carol is very demonstrative and upbeat.
Dr. Greg Roberts
Burlington, ON

The workshop was so helpful in helping me know how to relate to other personality types in building the business. I now see why some people may have been overwhelmed by my approach. I loved being able to see myself and what my strengths and weaknesses are.
Lorinda Dyck
Burlington, ON

This is an excellent, interactive workshop. There were different ways of learning, self awareness and development. Carol is a dynamic presenter. I loved the role playing, the audience input, the handouts and the excellent presenter.
Rose Price
London, ON

It was amazing to see and hear the people in my group that all felt the same. I had never categorized people like that before. I know it will be useful in my business.
Helen Ellersdorfer
Burlington. ON

Great information! This workshop was a very helpful tool for becoming adaptable to different personality types. The information on the different personality types was a great eye-opener on how to and how not to approach potential recruits, how to select partnerships to help your business succeed.
Barbara James,
North York, ON

The FOUR Core Networking Types

Dispelling the Myth that Only a Particular Type of
Person Can Succeed in Network Marketing

By

Carol Merlo, M.Ed.

Health, Wealth & Happiness, Inc.
2510 Brookforest Dr., Roanoke, TX 76262 USA
carol@networkingtypes.com 817-337-5659
www.networkingtypes.com

Published by Health, Wealth & Happiness, Inc.
Roanoke, Texas

Third Printing, April, 2008

ISBN No: 978-0-9814689-0-7

ACKNOWLEGEMENTS

Special thanks to my mother Ann Beveridge, who originally encouraged my interest in Psychology and introduced me to Personality Typing.

To my dear friends, Marion Head, Phil and Kathleen Peters, Bob Phillips, Bob Panico, Christine Detrick, and Peggy H. MacKinnon Bendell for their attention to detail and valuable feedback in making this book more complete, understandable and impactful.

Finally, to my amazing husband Bill, who always cares enough to look deeply into my material, ask pertinent questions, and improve the quality of my work. Without his love and care, this book would not have been possible.

Be the Leader You Would Follow

Why You Need to Learn this Information

If you are in the Network Marketing business, your objective is to find people who want to improve their financial, interpersonal, and/or physical condition in life and to teach them how to achieve their goals through your vehicle. This is a wonderful dream and yet many people fail before they even begin because they do not understand this business model and so believe they don't have either the right type of personality or the skills to achieve success in this business.

Many people erroneously think that you have to be a strong sales person, a high-powered promoter, or an extreme extravert to be successful in this business. Often we look to the interesting 'life of the party' or the strong, charismatic leader as our role model and, from the failed attempt to become that person, we simply give up before we begin.

The truth is that all types of people become great Network Marketers. Anyone who has the desire, determination, and self-discipline to consistently reach out to people and offer them the opportunity can succeed in sharing a great product and opportunity.

We are all uniquely different, but we are not so different from one another that general principles about how to approach, teach, and motivate different types people can't be found and applied. The key is to find either the greatest common denominator or greatest number of characteristics that are common to groups of people and then learn how to apply those commonalities to our recruiting and retention efforts.

Historically, quadrant personality typing has been the easiest way to achieve an understanding of the differences and the commonalities between people. It has been used effectively to approach, motivate, and educate people throughout history.

I am sure you have been exposed to it in one form or another. People ascribe colors, animal names, or jewels to the types to make their approaches seem to be unique. Nevertheless, the basic four types are essentially the same in each of these methods.

My purpose in writing this book is for you to easily and simply identify various types of people and relate to them in a way that works for them so that you can improve the quality of your business and relationship. This is a simple process but it isn't always easy. Learning new behaviors takes an investment of time and energy but it is well worth it.

The Skills Needed to Become a World Class Network Marketer

Are certain people 'better' at Network Marketing than others are? Certainly! However, those people had to learn those skills somewhere in life in order to apply them to this business. People rarely arrive with all of the skills required to build a large business. For most people, it's a 'learn as you grow' phenomenon. If this is your vehicle and you are hoping to become world-class at it, get ready to adapt and learn.

In order to sell something effectively, you need to understand why a person would buy what you have and then develop the skills that will enhance the probability of enabling that person to receive your information and make a buying decision.

Many of us make the mistake of basing our opportunity presentation on what interested us originally instead of taking the time to learn about the other person and find out how our product or service can meet their needs. If we want to experience success in Network Marketing, we must understand that our own interests are best served when we can convey the quality, consistency, and value of a product in such a way that the person sees their WIIFM (what's in it for me).

This becomes particularly important when we are dealing with a long-term endeavor like a Network Marketing enterprise, where the relationship you are creating with each contact can become life-long, so is very important.

It is also important to understand that whether we are dealing with sales, friendships, or even mates, we go through a filtering and selection process to make decisions, regardless of which personality type we have. Therefore, when we are sharing something with someone, we need to match our information and communication style to his or hers so they can more effectively receive it.

From that point, we can determine if the product or service is a good fit for both that person and for ourselves. However, if we can't get behind the 'firewall' of their personality, that person won't be able to make an effective decision.

No matter which type you are, this business will cause you to develop skills that you don't currently have and build on your innate strengths. In this book, you will discover that each person, regardless of his or her type, is innately gifted with some of these skills and is weak at others. Although you can develop each of these skills as you grow, be on the lookout for others who are naturally better where you are weak and team up with them.

To become great at this, you will need to develop five basic skills. First, you need to hire, partner with, or become an effective recruiter/promoter. Unless you have lots of money, an automated advertising campaign, and a product that sells itself, you will need to influence people.

Through trial and error, you can develop the skill to contact, engage, present to, and enroll people. If you are not willing to do this, even poorly — at first — you will not get very far. You need to have people buying your products in order to receive income.

Second, you need to hire, partner with, or become someone to do the follow up and relationship building. Some recruiters are great at 'getting them in' but they fail at 'keeping them in' because there was no relationship or caring established in the initial interaction. It's a rare product that produces loyalty without requiring a consistent, caring person to follow through with the end consumer.

Third, you need to hire, partner with, or become a person (or have a system) that can train people how to do the above. Many recruiters can 'do it' but don't know how to 'duplicate' success. Therefore, we need to have someone who can create a system that everyone can follow and, once the system is in place, effectively train people to follow it.

Although many companies have trainers who can provide this service for the entire field organization, everyone will need to develop some training and communication skills to get their people focused on the path. Training involves more than providing sales aids and websites. Consistent conference calls, training meetings and one on ones grow a team.

Fourth, you need to hire, partner with, or become a person that can organize the office, respond to and organize emails, keep track of the promotional materials, the inventory, the downline analyses, and pay the bills. This requires an entirely different set of skills because they aren't people skills but rather data skills. Without a good organizer, an organization may fall apart because people will fall through the cracks. I have found very few excellent, open, people-oriented types who can also stay organized, maintain good records and create or print downline reports. Therefore, they need to have an organizer on their team.

Finally, you need to hire, partner with, or become a mentor and accountability partner, a person who can see the best in your people better than they can see it themselves. As such, you will inspire them to do those things necessary to succeed, even if it means that they will be a little uncomfortable or afraid in the process. As you develop Leaders under you, this will increasingly become your role.

<u>No one comes into this business with all of the above skills mastered and we will always be better at some of the skills than others.</u>

Network Marketing is so dynamic because it is like living inside a personal development program. It requires continuous growth and development in order to master it.

As you apply the material in this book, you will begin to notice the natural inclinations and skills of the various types of people that come into your organization and into your life. Once you become adept at recognizing and understanding personality types, you will learn to relate to people from *their* point of view. This will help them excel at their natural inclinations to develop those skills that they aren't versed in to create a great team. This book will teach you the elements you need to build that team.

List the Five Skills Needed to Become a World Class Network Marketing Leader

1. _____

2. _____

3. _____

4. _____

5. _____

The Elements of a Great Team

You might be thinking, "if only I could be more open, friendly, influential, persuasive, and knowledgeable, I would be more successful at this business". Well, there is more to the story…

Roger is one of those people that you might think you would want to have in your group. He has personally recruited over 400 people into his downline. He has won every incentive the company has offered, shows up at all the main events, and any time you talk to him, he is excited about the company and his future in it.

The problem? He hasn't ever gone past the lowest leadership level and does not enjoy a residual income from his business. Roger sells the products easily and has no problem selling the biggest pack. He is motivated by winning trips and incentives. But, that's where it ends. Roger doesn't follow up, build relationships, or support others to share the opportunity.

Those of us who are not like Roger think, "if only I could be like him…then I would be successful at this". Well, in Roger's case, that's just not enough to make a successful team.

The interesting thing is that Roger might be thinking, "if only I could be more organized and do more follow up, then I could be really great at this".

This misconception about the success of strong recruiters in our business permeates our beliefs to the point that many of the people you will introduce this to will say, "I'm not a salesman type. I would never be any good at this", and they will not even try!

These people overlook many opportunities because they don't understand the importance of appreciating *who they actually are*. As a result, they don't develop their strengths or find those people who can complement their weaknesses with the skills to build a strong team and a successful organization.

I love to tell people that network marketing is a team sport. Our business model is built upon the foundation of mutual benefit. This is very different from the usual corporate hierarchical model where opportunities for promotion are limited so competition and exclusivity are rampant. Whereas, in network marketing, people can't succeed in their business unless they can help others succeed in theirs.

As a Leader, I must consistently convey that I work for my people; that they don't work for me. Consequently, I must create a trusting relationship with my team so they will feel confident and safe in asking for help and training because this might be the first time in their business career where they actually become a part of a cooperative team.

Answering the 'Who am I' Question

I can remember the first time I became aware of my *self*. I was 11 years old and was standing under a basketball hoop on the playground at school. It was like coming out of a dream into the real world for the first time. As I looked up at the strings on the hoop, I realized that I was a *self*, unique and independent of any other *self*. I was 'Me'. This was a lonely, yet freeing experience.

That was when I came to realize that I have independent thought and could make my own decisions; I did not have to do what my parents or teachers said and could make decisions based on my beliefs and interests. (I later learned that the brain goes through various cognitive stages as it matures, and this was just a new stage in my development.)

This experience was so profound for me that over the next few years I read as much as I could about 'who am I' and personal development. This grew into a lifetime love of psychology. I was driven by the need to understand people and put their behavior into perspective. I wanted to make friends and be popular, so I read as much as I could to figure out how to do this. (Ironically, the more popular people were doing, rather than reading).

This is what I learned:

To be effective at personal development we need to understand the difference between the things we can change about our personalities (our characteristics or 'state') and the things we can't (our temperament or 'traits').

We typically think of personality as a combination of attitudes, beliefs, sense of humor, moods, speaking style, gestures, and mannerisms. Most of us sense that we are born with some inherent personality traits that are the result of our biological genetic coding, which determines how our personality expresses itself. These traits form our involuntary habits, determine our preferred way of gathering information and influence the choice of words we use to communicate with others, as well as how we learn. While that is probably true, it is difficult to attribute genetic factors to personality. Current scientific research has so far shown that only child disinhibition (how inhibited, or introverted, you are) has been shown to be a significant predictor of adult personality characteristics.

What this means from a physiological standpoint, is that some people have a predisposition for higher levels of physiological arousal to environmental stimuli, which includes our responses when exposed to and interacting with people. Because of this, such people develop inhibitions, which make them more shy and uneasy in social situations. I like to call this quality *inherent sensitivity*.

In contrast to the inherent qualities, the learned components of personality are called characteristics. Our characteristics reflect the behavioral patterns we develop from the decisions we have made as a response to our life experiences. Our characteristics differentiate us from others, and establish how we express our identities to the outside world. Our characteristics are responsible for the formation of habits, comfort zones, quirks, and idiosyncratic behavioral patterns

Traits + Characteristics = Personality Type

Think of your personality type as your automatic pilot. It creates the involuntary behavioral patterns necessary for you to function and survive. Your type is your own personal road map that guides you toward the outward direction you take in life. Its characteristics influence what you become. It affects your self-image, self-esteem, self-confidence, and self-worth. It motivates you, creates your irritations, and controls stress and how that stress affects you. It is not a self-fulfilling prophesy, however.

Personality influences the way you face life's challenges and how you cope with them. It is the organizing principle that affects your sense of reality and spirituality. It greatly influences your health and overall sense of well-being.

To a large extent we can change our attitudes, thoughts, feelings, and behaviors. Because most people have formed their personalities by adulthood, re-forming them on a significant level is exceptionally challenging but with work, we can adapt to match the characteristics of others when communicating and relating.

You *can* control your characteristics and beliefs. *Characteristics*, in contrast to *traits*, are changeable.

Motivational trainers and psychotherapists all know that we have the ability to change habits, thoughts, and behaviors through intention and practice, but because we have certain inborn traits and impulses, some things will never change about us. Efforts to do so have resulted in emotional pain, mental illness, self-loathing, and even suicide because people decide that they aren't 'good enough' the way they are.

One of the biggest errors people make in personality typing is that they assume they are a certain type because they believe who they actually are is somehow wrong or inadequate.

People usually attempt to change their God-given traits because they did not receive adequate attention, affection, or approval from the people who were important to them when they were children.

In fact, many people don't ever actualize their true selves because of the influences of parents, institutions, or other factors that suppress them in an effort to control them and make them fit in to a particular social model.

The recognition of and development into becoming who we actually are, in contrast to who we are currently being, is a process that most people address as they grow into leadership in Network Marketing. Personal development programs are plentiful in our business and fill this important need.

One of the primary benefits of Network Marketing is having the opportunity to grow and develop into who we actually are in a supportive and nurturing environment. Network Marketing is one of the few vocations that encourages personal and leadership development, social skills, and self esteem building. I have seen people transformed through the process of building a successful downline. People who were shy and afraid become confident and courageous. People who were negative and critical become open and trusting.

So, as you read this, remember that people can change much of whom they are *being* in the world but certain behavioral styles and talents will remain fixed throughout a lifetime. It is our job to accept and love that in ourselves and in others if we want to experience serenity.

What I Can Change About Myself (character)

_____

_____

_____

_____

What I Can't Change About Myself (traits)

_____

_____

_____

_____

Discovering Your Type

Quadrant personality typing typically assesses where a person is on two dimensions, and then places that person's type into a box. The next section will introduce you to the various dimensions that determine types. You can also take the free online personality test at www.networkingtypes.com to help you determine your type.

We will use the following dimensions to determine the four core types:

1. Whether you are people or task oriented
2. Whether you are outward or inward focused in your thinking and behavior
3. Your primary business orientation
4. Which basic outcome drives your behavior

There Is No Right or Wrong Place to Be

Imagine you are in a room full of people who all want to learn about their type. First, let's divide everyone into one of two groups — the people who are people-oriented or the people who are task-oriented. This is the first dimension upon which we determine types.

People-Oriented	Task-Oriented

Friendly, Warm	Reserved, Formal
Likes to touch when talking	Keeps a personal 'space'
Easily shares feelings	Keeps feelings private
Relaxed about time	Disciplined about time
Spontaneous	Prefers to plan
Uses feeling words	Uses thinking words

Pauline, a terrific Leader, is married to a dynamic business builder named Terry. Each of them contributes value to their business in a complementary way. Terry is a person who immediately puts people at ease when they are around him. He is easy to be with. People feel comfortable around him.

Although Pauline cares deeply for people, her passion is in accomplishing tasks. People don't immediately feel comfortable around her. She feels great when everything comes out on time, when the bases are covered and when everything is 'done'. Pauline is Task-Oriented.

Task-Oriented people like everything spelled out and clear. People-Oriented people are more tolerant of ambiguity. People-Oriented people like to have options and don't want to be constrained by time, commitment, or definition. Task-Oriented people like to have targets, mean what they say, and say what they mean, which includes being on time and valuing sequence.

Task-Oriented people want the job done, so will sacrifice the feelings of others if it means they can accomplish the goal. These people have a strong ability to categorized, itemize, plan, and execute tasks and objectives and sometimes see people as being in the way of the accomplishment of a task.

People-Oriented people, however, are more interested in the relationships they create. They are interested in the outcome, of course, but they have a much more refined sense of what another person is feeling, and typically will create alliances to get their goals accomplished. They tend to be more relaxed and easy-going, will take time to converse and laugh, even if it means that the job may not be done on time.

<u>Where are you on this continuum?</u>

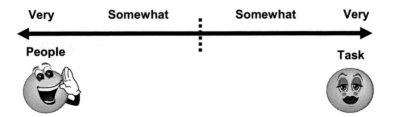

Next, let's divide the people in the room by a different characteristic; whether they are more Outward or Inward focused.

Outward   **Inward**

Talks first	Waits to be approached
Decisive	Slower to decide
Expressive	Sensitive
Impatient	Patient
Opinionated	Reserved
Makes it happen	Experiences it happen

Outward people become impatient more easily than Inward people do. Inward people don't like to be rushed. Depending on their type, they will either be more concerned about the person or about accuracy than making quick decisions.

To a great extent, the degree to which you are Outward or Inward was hard-wired into you. Although you can modify your behavior to adapt, your tendency when too hungry, angry, lonely, or tired (under stress) will be to move toward your natural inclination.

In a business that demands reaching out to others, many Inward people believe that they can't do this business. Inward people are usually more sensitive to the behaviors of others and can get overwhelmed easily, so can readily take on this false belief.

It requires a lot of energy for an Inward person to be outgoing. Introverted people have higher levels of physiological arousal, so they are easily conditioned by environmental stimuli. Because of this, they develop more inhibitions, which make them more shy and uneasy in social situations.

Inward people like to know the precise steps, scripts, and processes in order to recruit people. Because it is not natural for them to be assertive, they need a structure to depend on. If they are provided with a script and structure, they can learn to duplicate success and become good Leaders.

Where are *you* on this continuum? When entering a room full of people, do you feel happy and energized or uncomfortable and shy? Are you soft spoken or are you boisterous? Are you on the extreme end of the continuum or closer to the middle?

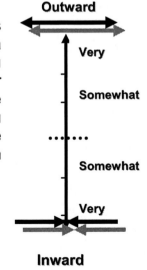

Outward

Very

Somewhat

Somewhat

Very

Inward

Put Yourself into this Grid

Now, as we add names to these quadrants you will see personality types emerge.

If you are Outward and People-Oriented you are an Entertainer. If you are Outward and Task-Oriented, you are a Captain. If you are Inward and People-Oriented, you are an Angel. If you are Inward and Task-Oriented, you are a Professor.

Outward
Talks first, Decisive, Expresses Opinions, Impatient, Makes it happen

People-Oriented
Friendly, Warm
Likes to Touch
Shares feelings
Relaxed about time
Spontaneous
Uses Feeling Words

The Entertainer

The Captain

Task-Oriented
Reserved, Formal
Keeps a personal 'space'
Keeps feelings private
Disciplined about time
Prefers to plan
Uses Thinking Words

The Angel

The Professor

Inward
Waits to be approached, Slow to decide, Reserves Opinions, Patient, Experiences it happen

My Primary Type is

_____

Unsure of your Type?

Don't worry if you can't completely fit yourself into a specific box. We are all unique and no two of us has the same combination of these characteristics.

There are infinite combinations of personality types. Imagine that the four squares below are overlaid by a grid, which contains billions of points. Each of us is somewhere on this grid. You might end up in the middle of two types, on the far extreme of a type, or very close to the center.

As you can see from the graphic below, as we get closer to the middle, the types merge into shades of gray.

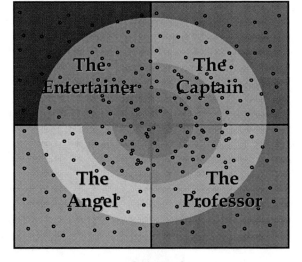

Outward

The Entertainer

The Captain

People

Task

The Angel

The Professor

Inward

You may also notice that people will change their behaviors depending upon their level of freedom, security, and comfort in a situation. For example, if you were an outgoing, warm, and fun Entertainer but were forced to live in a concentration camp where being noticed could get you killed, you would become subdued. Over time, your personality would change. Similarly, if a child has a strong tendency toward a type but the parents don't value that type, a child will attempt to be different and modify his style in order to receive approval and love.

Remember, very few qualities are in-born, so we can change who we are being in the world.

I believe that the freedom to be authentic comes from being in a supportive environment where an individual can express his gifts and experience successes, as a result. Fortunately, network marketing affords one the opportunity to focus on our gifts and express our true selves as we grow in our businesses.

Many people that attend my workshops put themselves into the wrong type, particularly when they believe that their type will not provide the recognition, results, relationships, or rationale they are seeking. From the outside, it's relatively easy to tell if a person is people or task, outward or inward. From the inside, our judgments about who we are can prevent us from seeing ourselves as we actually are.

The Subtypes

We typically fall into a major type and then a subtype. Each of the four quadrants has four subtypes. Depending on where you are in the grid, you will incorporate the characteristics of second personality type and become a blend.

So, you will find that people who are not on the extreme outer corners of a type will see themselves in two boxes:

Angels can be:
Relating Angels   Thinking Angels
Directing Angels   Influencing Angels

Entertainers can be:
Relating Entertainers   Thinking Entertainers
Directing Entertainers   Influencing Entertainers

Professors can be:
Relating Professors   Thinking Professors
Directing Entertainers   Influencing Entertainers

Captains can be:
Relating Captains   Thinking Captains
Relating Captains   Influencing Captains

My secondary type is_____

If you are still unsure of your type, think about how you were as a child or what you are like when you are completely relaxed and feeling confident about yourself.

You may express different qualities at home than at your job. Think about areas in your life where you feel the most confident and comfortable and notice who you are in those situations.

Ask some of your closest friends how they see you. Remember, becoming who you actually are is a life-long process.

Pick the type that is least like you first.

Personal development programs can help you discover your innate gifts and enhance your skills at the same time.

How We Act When Under Stress

People-oriented people will typically withdraw from situations that involve conflict to preserve relationships, whereas task-oriented people will attack to force results, even if it means being passive-aggressive. Task-oriented people experience greater pressure to achieve when under stress so will push to get a job done, and risk alienating people, whereas the people-oriented type will withdraw from people to find a solution and spare others' feelings.

The Entertainer seeks recognition by using persuasion and sociability. When he is not recognized, he will become indifferent and uncaring.

The Captain seeks results by controlling the environment. When she can't get the results she wants on time, she will become insensitive and hurt peoples' feelings.

The Professor will become critical when he can't experience a rationale for something despite his best efforts to plan.

The Angel will become indecisive and withdraw when she can't create a relationship by harmonizing with another.

The graphic on the following page shows how stressors or conflict can affect each type.

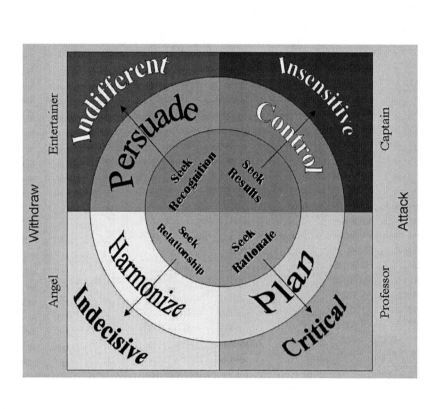

Personality Types, Leadership and the Art of War

I spent my childhood in libraries, in nature, and in the classroom where I felt comfortable in the world of theory. I loved doing science experiments and had a good sense of music, so learned the guitar and sang. In school, I would fall asleep while listening to history and political science. I didn't like battles and guns. To me, these topics were 'stupid'. I also didn't want to have anything to do with business or finance. After all, I was an artist!

Therefore, I was unprepared to take care of myself when I got out of school. I was inept when it came to doing banking or negotiating a job interview to earn a living and rise in the world of business. It took most of my early adulthood to figure out that art must become a business if you want to eat, and businesses are run using the same skills as those used in politics, sports, and war.

In graduate school, I started reading business management books and discovered that there is a common terminology regarding leadership styles among business theorists, team sports, and the military.

This terminology is similar because every economic endeavor requires the same types of leadership styles in the utilization of people and energy. War games predominate in business and sports. Therefore, if you want to succeed in Network Marketing, it is important to understand the mechanisms of winning a battle, even if you are an artist like me!

The next dimension we want to look at is how a person leads in business (or war). Although Network Marketing is a business model based on *cooperation* rather than *competition*, you need the same methodologies, whether it's to win a battle or to create a successful organization.

Each of these methodologies is naturally correlated with one of the four core personality types:

- **The Entertainer is *Tactical***
- **The Captain is *Logistical***
- **The Angel is *Diplomatic***
- **The Professor is *Strategic***

As you are reading the following methodologies, think of how you typically lead your team in your Network Marketing business. This will help you refine your identification of your type.

Strategy – The Why

A strategy is an overall plan, method, or series of maneuvers for obtaining a specific goal or result. The most effective battles are won when a good strategy has been formulated first.

Strategic thinking is extremely valuable in determining the direction in which your business goes in order to accomplish your 'Why'. Strategic Leadership involves the ability to anticipate, prepare, and position your team for the future.

In Network Marketing, we often call our business plans a 'system.' Our Professors are typically the system builders. If an organization has too many systems, people will be distracted, moving from one thing to another in an attempt to succeed. Therefore, a single, clear, sequential system is necessary to guide people to success. Usually the Professors will create the systems but will not be the implementers of those systems. They will leave that to the Captains and Entertainers.

If you are new in Network Marketing, make sure you are following a system that has been proven, allows for the changes that occur as a business grows, and is not dependent upon a specific individual for it to work. Also, be wary of organizations that change their system too often. This causes confusion in the field and inhibits duplication.

Logistics – The How

Logistics takes the system and focuses on the planning, implementation, and coordination of the business, which includes the overall management of how resources are moved to the areas where they are required. Logistical Leadership *assumes the 'Why'* and is more interested in the 'How', or implementation method of the strategy. Logistics is vital to the success of any project. Using logistics you can have the right people in the right places at the right times to accomplish the best results.

A logistical leader can easily determine the timing needed in all areas from getting tools to distributers and setting up conference calls, to knowing when to follow up. They will be able to devise training sequences and ensure people will get to events by providing information through emails, phone calls, and websites.

Do not assume logistics is a passive activity! Logistics is the driver, directing our businesses to make them grow more efficiently and effectively. The Captain, as a logistical Leader, will give you the Strategist's map, give you the steps to follow, train you, and hold you accountable for meeting your goals, too.

Don't expect a lot of sympathy, however. Logistics is all about task management and implementation of the system. If you want results, follow the logistical leader's directions.

Tactics – The When and Where

Tactics involves making moves to better one's position -- where the action currently is -- to achieve a goal. A good tactician will scan for opportunities, look for the best angle of approach, and come up with a plan of immediate action for the greatest advantage.

Tactics for Entertainers involves persuasion, promotion, artistry, and improvisation. They can turn on a dime and have fun at the same time. They are inspirational and full of ideas.

The strategy can be there and the logistics can have been done to get a room and have a presenter, but the acquisition of the audience is necessary to make it all work. A good tactical leader will provide a list of ways to contact, present, and gather business builders. They are full of great ideas. It's up to the logistical leader, however, to help you determine which tactic is best for you.

Diplomacy – The Who

Remember Roger who was a terrific recruiter and didn't have a team, despite all his sign ups? Well, Roger needs a few diplomats on his team. Any endeavor can go awry if the relationships between the members of the team aren't built and maximized or even if communications with the leader of the 'opposing team' fail. The diplomat is the relationship builder and peacemaker.

The Angel as a diplomatic leader enhances team loyalty and commitment, which is essential to the survival of any organization in today's competitive, global economy.

Diplomatic leaders have the innate ability to put personal feelings aside, avoid anger, and by doing so are highly successful in resolving conflicts. People love diplomats.

Follow up, relationship building, and people skills in general are the glue that holds an organization together. Angels, as natural diplomats, are typically the ones to build a long-term business with loyal associates.

<u>Circle Your Most Natural Business Orientation</u>

Strategy   **Tactics**

Logistics   **Diplomacy**

Which is your most natural orientation? Typically, each person is uniquely gifted in one of the four, which corresponds to their personality type.

The Fundamental Drive of Each of the FOUR Core Networking Types

The final dimension we want to look at is the underlying emotional need or drive of each of the types. Each type has a unique need that they are trying to fill. Our job is to recognize that need and help them fill it. When you can help a person feel great about who they are, you are more likely to maintain that relationship and build a strong, enduring business. In fact, people will express negative, critical, or self-destructive behaviors when they don't have the opportunity to fulfill their basic drive.

- **Entertainers crave *Recognition***
- **Captains crave *Results***
- **Angels crave *Relationship***
- **Professors crave *Rationale***

One of the biggest mistakes both sales people and networkers make is to provide people with the wrong answer to a need. Clearly, asking questions is fundamental to determining type and providing a solution to the underlying emotional need of an individual.

When you fulfill what that individual wants and needs you will create loyalty in your group and empower more people to become leaders.

Personality Type Summary Graphic

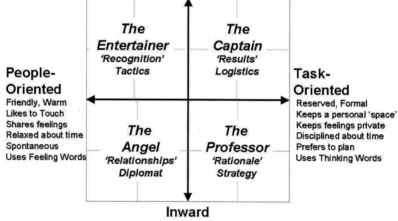

Outward
Talks first, Decisive, Expressive, Impatient, Opinionated,
Makes it happen

People-Oriented
Friendly, Warm
Likes to Touch
Shares feelings
Relaxed about time
Spontaneous
Uses Feeling Words

The Entertainer
'Recognition'
Tactics

The Captain
'Results'
Logistics

Task-Oriented
Reserved, Formal
Keeps a personal 'space'
Keeps feelings private
Disciplined about time
Prefers to plan
Uses Thinking Words

The Angel
'Relationships'
Diplomat

The Professor
'Rationale'
Strategy

Inward
Waits to be approached, Slow to decide, Sensitive
Patient, Wants to be liked, Experiences it happen

How Do I Apply this Information?

By using the above chart, you not only have the means to determine *your* personality type but also that of others at a very basic level. On the next several pages, you will learn to become an expert at identifying and dealing with each of them and I have provided a handy 'cheat sheet' at the end, which you can tear out and take with you to help you determine types.

Let me tell you why developing this one skill is so important to your success in life…

In order to succeed in this business, <u>you will need to understand that you *can* develop the skills to build this business regardless of which type you are.</u> This will take continuous effort and connection to your 'Why'.

You will need to re-read and study this book and apply these skills until it becomes second nature to recognize the different types and adjust your approach to relate to them. Is it worth it? Let me tell you what this information did for me…

Once I figured out that I was a Thinking Captain, I had to come to terms with the liabilities involved in that and see the *value* in being a who I am, as well. I had had the mistaken idea that only Entertainers were any good at all in this business so everyone should be like them.

Because I wasn't as good at people skills as I was at task skills, I naturally wanted to improve in my weak areas. This wasn't easy but it was necessary to accomplish my goal of being an effective leader in my business and to help others become successful.

I did lots of personal development work to become better at my people skills and made a lot of mistakes along the way. I was determined to succeed so was willing to pick myself up and try again each time I didn't perform to my standards, hurt someone's feelings or lost an associate.

But what I had been missing until recently was that when I can determine someone else's type, I can adapt my approach, meet their needs more effectively, and be more successful because I am more effective at communicating and dealing with people in a style that relates to their personality. It wasn't so much about changing my type as relating to other types comfortably by changing my approach to meet their needs.

I now have the confidence that I know how to interact with others. When I am working with Angels I can spend a few minutes chatting with them about their life, being interested in their feelings, and asking open-ended questions before I get down to the bottom line. Because I am a Captain, and crave results, the result I am looking for is a good relationship, so will take the time to do this.

When I am dealing with Professors or Angels, I can expect to have more than one conversation to get them engaged in my opportunity and product. I get to relax and not be concerned if they aren't interested the first time because I understand their need for follow up.

When I am dealing with Entertainers, I can speed up, get excited, and be ready to have fun. I can focus on *them* and make them feel important by listening, laughing, and enjoying their stories without being concerned about the accuracy of their details. Moreover, I don't have to be upset when they are late. Instead, I can anticipate that and either be a little late myself or bring a book.

With Captains, I can quickly provide what they need to make a decision to move business forward. I can provide information they can use to create results and make quick decisions. I can provide them with what they need to help me so we can both get results that are more effective in our businesses.

Which people on your team are innately gifted in skills that you can help develop to make a better contribution to your entire team? Who else do you need on your team in order to fill the gaps so you can have a dynamic organization?

Who are the great recruiters on your team? If you are good at follow up, help them by creating relationships with their people. If you are great at getting people in, find someone who is good at relationships and build underneath them. If you are great with people and your office is a mess, get an organizer to help you and build underneath them.

If you are a good trainer, see who you can find that needs your help to build their business while they help you build yours.

Find those people whose strengths will complement your weaknesses. Finally, find, follow, or create a system that can guide you and your people to success.

As you go through the following pages, don't just read the detail of the types; jot down the names of people you know.

Make notes and think about how you can relate to them better with the information you are learning.

Keep practicing as you meet new people. Soon you will develop a love for each of the best qualities of each type as you have fun with it.

The FOUR Core Networking Types in Detail

What follows is a general description of each type — how they act, how they sound, what drives them, and how to sell to them. Now, you may see yourself in one of the types but don't feel you quite fit. That is normal. Remember the billions of points in the quadrants? No two human beings are exactly alike, so we are looking for tendencies, rather than absolutes here.

Entertainers

- People-Oriented
- Outward
- Recognition Driven
- Tactical Leaders

I ran into Melody at a party recently. Her personality type is easy to spot. She shows up late because she had a lot to do before she came and got a little lost on the way. She walks into the room with a queenly air and just knows the party wasn't complete until her arrival. She is dressed in bright colors; you can hear her laughter from across the room, even with the music playing and the sounds of other partygoers close by.

She walks up to the first person she sees and introduces herself with a flourish. She immediately starts talking about herself in a friendly way and usually makes everyone laugh very quickly.

She talks a lot and most people may not get a word in edgewise unless they interrupt her. It usually takes her a bit longer to tell a story because it has lots of embellishments and personal anecdotes in it.

Robbie comes in. He is an extreme Entertainer. Robbie hugs everyone he talks to in the room and says something funny. He always has a group of people around him and loves being the center of attention. He has lots of influence and is always #1. Everyone loves Robbie!

Entertainers never meet a stranger. They lend electricity to the environment and to the people around them. They live life at the level of a gourmet feast and they bring to work and play a sense that something delicious is about to happen. Wherever they are, the atmosphere takes on a glow, seems brighter, more colorful and charged with an excitement that others often admire and even envy.

For an Entertainer, to be without impact or to make no difference in human affairs is what Tony Allesandra says is like being 'deprived of oxygen'. They hunger to make a splash, make something happen, to have a piece of the action, and to hit the big time.

Why You Need an Entertainer on Your Team

Entertainers are the best tacticians because they live in the present and see opportunities in events and people that strategists and logistical people may overlook.

How to Recognize an Entertainer

Word Usage

- Will include you in the conversation
- Tell stories and jokes
- *Here's an idea…*
- *I feel this is the way to…*
- *Tell me what you think about…*
- *My sense is that…*
- Switches from one topic to another easily
- Words are more about people than about things

Vocal

- Speaks fast
- Variety in inflection
- Vary pitch of their speech

Visual

- Facially animated
- Lots of hand gestures
- Spontaneous touching
- Big hand shakes
- Can't sit still

Key Qualities

- Impressed by recognition, excitement, and other outgoing people
- Love to have fun
- Like to avoid conflict
- Get bored easily
- Quick due to impatience
- Motivated by the ability to influence others

- Talk about themselves
- Not detail oriented
- Make decisions too quickly without much thought
- Optimistic
- Not good at follow through

What Drives an Entertainer?

Little Judy sashays into a room full of adults. She announces loudly that she can do cartwheels and wants everyone to watch her. 'Look at me, look at me', she says. Entertainers are driven by 'look at me', too. They want to be noticed and in the spotlight. It's difficult to sit and listen. Like children, they 'just want to have fun'. If an activity doesn't appear to be fun relatively quickly, an Entertainer will get bored and either move to another activity or create a situation that causes fun to happen.

Entertainers continuously seek approval and are motivated by accolades, especially if that approval is public.

Entertainers are at the center of influence in most Network Marketing organizations. The opportunity to be in the spotlight, influence people, and have fun without time constraints or the confinement of the corporate setting makes the MLM industry an ideal business model for this type.

How Entertainers Build the Business

- They just wing it, start talking to everyone enthusiastically and let the Upline or an assistant do the registrations and ordering online.
- They don't need to know the details of the products or plan to get people interested.
- They have a good time at all the meetings and events and make some new friends as they interrupt others to tell stories and show off their new associates.
- They can have huge parties that everyone attends because they all know how much fun it will be.
- Everyone will be talking about what a great person that Entertainer is!

Here is how an Entertainer would talk to a prospect in a sampling program:

"So, which gift do you want to try? Let me know how you feel, honey. I can't wait to tell Jerry I ran into you!"

Notice that there is enthusiasm in the Entertainer's language. Because they are people-oriented, they will use feeling words, rather than thinking words and they will usually connect one person to another, using their name.

The underlying message you get when listening to the Entertainer is, "*So... where do we go from here? I know you are going to just love this!*"

The Four Subtypes of Entertainers

Influencing Entertainer

- Friendly and fun. Life of the party.
- Needs recognition to maintain energy
- Optimistic and happy
- Will start activities but not finish them
- Avoids detail and conflicts

Directing Entertainer

- Highly resourceful
- Persuasive
- Has a large network of contacts
- Can delegate and take charge
- Doesn't follow through

Relating Entertainer

- Charming
- Sees life as an exciting drama
- Empathetic and overly subjective
- Great at getting people together
- Gets bored easily

Thinking Entertainer

- Inspirational and enthusiastic
- Impulsive
- Fascinating conversationalist
- Can improvise easily
- Takes on too many projects

Recruiting an Entertainer

- Talk about how easy and fun it will be to do this.
- Emphasize how your product or opportunity will provide recognition, and excitement.
- Act upbeat and enthusiastic.
- Be brief and allow for flexibility.
- Tell stories instead of relating facts.
- Show the big picture, not the details.
- Ask an open-ended closing question like, "Where do we go from here?"
- They will respond well to 'everyone's doing it' or 'this offer will expire soon.'
- They might over-buy and have buyer's remorse, so be sure to help them make a decision that they won't regret later.

After the Registration

- Send them the details of the transaction but be willing to do the registration for them and oversee their purchases.
- This type is most likely to regret a purchase or get bored, so remind them that they made the right choice.
- Show them new ways to use the products and be sure they are using the products correctly. They probably didn't read the directions.
- Have regular up beat social interactions with them in a relaxed setting.

Captains

- Task-Oriented
- Outward
- Results Driven
- Logistical Leaders

The company brings a team of top Leaders together to help create a new sales system. Derrick made sure he was part of this group because he knows that he has all the answers and without him, the whole system will fail.

He is not afraid to step on some toes and make sure the company runs right. He can hurt some feelings without paying too much attention and doesn't consider that much of a problem. He talks fast and rarely says something designed to nurture, encourage, or harmonize the group.

To Derrick, the group dynamic is not as important as the task at hand. He is passionate about making it work well and fast. He has already worked out the logistics and knows the best route to take, so expects to lead the way.

Derrick believes that most of the people on the team are irrelevant because he already has all the answers, and unless he has done some personal development work, he will consider having a team as unnecessary.

In fact, the majority of Derrick's ideas are sound and his uncanny sense of how to put methods and strategies together actually makes a better system for the company, despite his manner.

If you want a fast moving, goal-oriented and focused team, get a Captain. They are among the most competent and efficient people you can meet. They are so self directed that if you were to follow up with them for more than a brief 'touch base' they would be offended and think you thought they were incompetent.

Captains want all the control for themselves because they believe they can get it done right and on time. They don't want to take the risk of delegating the process to someone who may not do it as well or as quickly because they are very clear about how to accomplish the job effectively. Unfortunately, they can hurt some feelings and bruise some egos in the process.

This doesn't mean that Captains don't have feelings. Some are highly sensitive to rejection and simply don't understand that their behavior puts people off. The great Captains improve their people skills to get great results.

Captains like to have their accomplishments recognized by others.

Why You Need a Captain on Your Team

In Network Marketing, logistics is manifesteu ᴗ an ability to create a system of recruitment and training that perpetuates itself. Captains have the unique ability to see the goal and, at the same time, see what it takes in terms of skills, energy, and time needed to accomplish that goal. They make great Logistical Leaders.

How to Recognize a Captain

Word Usage
- *Tell me what the goal is*
- *I don't want excuses*
- *Write this down*
- Poor at small talk
- Won't state the obvious or repeat things
- Does not like to go from topic to topic without finishing one first
- Uses precise language

Vocal
- Intonation carries an implicit challenge
- May sound impatient but not actually feel that way.

Visual

- Firm handshake
- Emphatic
- Movements are fast, suggesting impatience and power
- Steady eye contact

Key Qualities

- Avoids the irrelevant and the redundant
- Quick-focused
- Loves accuracy, precision, and clarity
- Believe they can overcome any obstacle
- Can juggle lots of tasks and responsibilities and do them all well
- Act as if they are the only ones with the answer
- Decisive
- Time conscious
- Highly territorial
- Controlling

What Drives a Captain?

Captains are propelled by an inner need to be in charge. Because they believe they know the best and fastest way to accomplish things, they are highly sensitive to allowing others to take over and ruin it. The fear that it may be done poorly, late, or not at all compels the Captain to be in charge at all times. Trust in the outcome and in people is the Captain's ongoing challenge.

How Captains Build the Business

- They make a quick business plan, tell their Upline to back off, and do massive action using a proven marketing mechanism.
- They hold their team accountable to required team calls with associates who will provide a weekly progress report showing how many people they talked to, followed up with, and enrolled each day.
- They review their team's work and hold them accountable.
- This gives them control, yet still frees them to line up bigger challenges.
- Their teams grow quickly and competently!

Here's a typical way a Captain would hand out a sample:

"Look at the website so you can get in right away. I am giving you a gift of your choice of product to try so you can see how great they are. I want you to look at it right away and give me an answer."

Notice how you are given the impression that the Captain is very busy and doesn't want to spend very much time talking to the prospect? Sentences are filled with orders, rather than requests, and there are no stories, explanations or adjectives. The underlying feeling is "Tell me yes or tell me no, but tell me quick 'cause I've gotta go."

The Four Subtypes of Captains

Directing Captain

- Motivated by new opportunities
- Loves to give structure to organizations
- Likes to move on to new conquests
- Wants to have final say
- Takes charge of situations

Influencing Captain

- The most sociable of all the types
- Concerned with relationships as well as wanting to get things done
- Needs to feel appreciated for what he/she gives to others
- Does not like being told what to do

Relating Captain

- Charismatic
- Likes results more than people
- Likes to plan ahead
- Will cut corners to reach goals efficiently
- Driven to achieve

Thinking Captain

- Highly responsible
- Organizes orderly procedures
- Wants it done right and gets impatient with incompetence
- Loyal
- Goals and standards are higher than other types

Recruiting a Captain

- Show up on time.
- Do not give directions or orders.
- Allow them to control the sales process.
- Provide all the pertinent information they need to make their buying decision on the first meeting.
- Get to the bottom line, the logic behind it, and the reasons to make a decision quickly without too many details.
- Talk about the results they will get from using your product or being involved in your opportunity.
- Give them specific options for buying and make sure you have the data to back up each option, and then ask a qualifying question, like, "Which registration pack do you want?"
- Ask a closing question that can be answered with a Yes or No. You can ask, "Do you want to join our business?"

After the Registration

- Be sure to send them follow up information outlining your commitment to achieving results with them.
- Follow up often because they may go to a competitor.
- Ask if you delivered what you promised.
- Talk business.

Angels

- People-Oriented
- Inward
- Relationship Driven
- Diplomatic Leaders

Glenda shows up at the party with a warm smile on her face. She looks around at the people in the room to find someone she knows. Walking up she immediately establishes eye contact with her friend and asks a question that is personal but not invasive and then listens intently to her friend.

Glenda, like most Angels will talk with one person at a time to establish a feeling-based connection with them. She would never consider getting loud and would rather be off, engaged in one on one conversations with people. Glenda loves to include others in her vision by using tact and friendship as a way to encourage them to join her. She has the unique ability to be able to see the best in people and create teams that can accomplish projects easily and work well together.

Glenda is highly sensitive to the emotions of others and can enable her team by taking care of them too much, so not develop independent leaders.

Angels are soft spoken and casual. In conversation, they move from a few particulars to sweeping generalizations and jump from details to larger meanings. Because they are so people oriented, they will remember names easily and expect you to know the people whose names they mention.

Enthusiasm, which makes them full of life and awareness, is what characterizes an Angel. Their enthusiasm is based on something within themselves: an idea, mission, purpose, or passion. They want you to value, recognize and appreciate their 'true self.'

Because of their love of detail, you will notice that Angels will give you a blow by blow description any time they are telling a story. They want to be sure to tell you it was Wednesday, not Thursday, that they lost 4 pounds, not 5, or that it was in 1996 that Mary got her tonsils out.

Angels love the lengthy, intimate conversations and feel that the more details they know about you, the better they can fill your needs and take care of you.

Angels are nurturers and will often give gifts as an expression of appreciation and friendship. To feel fulfilled, they need to feel that they are making a difference and helping others to give them a sense of accomplishment.

Why You Need an Angel on Your Team

Angels are natural Diplomats and have tremendous skill in managing negotiations, handling people, etc., so that there is little or no ill will as a result. When people work together in harmony, they are more likely to enjoy the process of winning the war and Angels 'keep them in'.

They will follow up, make sure everyone gets to the meeting, bring the tools and food, and make sure everyone has a good time. They will know if anyone is having problems and has all the details about their families. They provide the glue that keeps the team together.

How to Recognize an Angel

Word Usage

- *Starts sentences with, "I feel"*
- *How is 'specific family member'?*
- *Let me help you*
- *I hope you don't mind if I…*
- *How will this affect people on a day-to-day level?*

Vocal

- Speaks slowly
- Soothing, even vocal tone
- Projects warmth and sincerity in their voice

Visual

- Balanced eye contact
- Hand shake is more tentative than strong

Key Qualities

- Empathetic
- Good listener
- Believes that goodness is everywhere in everything
- Trusts intuition more than the surroundings
- Loves stability
- Likes small groups of in-depth relationships
- Gets hurt feelings but won't tell you
- Doesn't rock the boat
- It's not whether you win or lose, it's how many friends you have that counts
- Seldom shows emotional peaks or valleys
- Doesn't like making big decisions
- Views actions as being louder than words
- Will avoid direct commands but will use illustrations and analogies to make a point

What Drives an Angel

Because Angels place people above tasks, they are driven to create harmony at all costs. Consequently, they see conflict as aversive and they will subordinate their own goals, interests, and activities to those of the people around them unless they work on assertiveness issues.

How Angels Build the Business

- They listen to their Upline at length about what exactly they should do and how to align together as they grow the business.
- They gather a loyal support team, and make sure they all have the cd's, literature, and presentation materials.
- After drawing up a step-by-step plan, they ask their people to work as a team, using the same system and tools.
- They see to it that everyone perseveres by encouraging, having frequent one on one conversations and being a good friend.
- Their business is built earnestly, methodically, and thoroughly and members of his team swear doing this business is the most fulfilling experience of their lives.

Here's how an Angel would sound when doing a sampling program:

"I want to make sure this is the right thing for you and your family. Do you think you would be ready to try one of these gifts? When can I get back with you to see how you feel?"

Notice that rather than commands, this language is filled with questions focused on the emotions of the prospect. The Angel does not want to hurt, rush or demand an answer from the prospect. The underlying feeling is "How do you feel about this so far?

The Four Subtypes of Angels

Relating Angel

- Easy to approach
- Cares deeply about a few special relationships or causes
- Does not like to attract attention
- Looks for ways to be of service
- Logic is optional

Directing Angel

- Driven and goal oriented
- Sets schedules and meets deadlines
- Makes sure things get done
- Enjoys being industrious
- Does not see the big picture

Influencing Angel

- Enjoys being around people but likes the focus to be on others
- Starts and sustains harmonious relationships
- Projects a warm, caring attitude
- Likes displays of affection and approval
- Does not plan or prepare

Thinking Angel

- Precise in thought and language
- Approaches new tasks cautiously
- Can detect contradictions easily
- Likes checklists
- Very detail oriented

Recruiting an Angel

- Break the ice with a brief personal comment.
- Ask about their family or service work.
- Mention the name of the person who referred you to them.
- Offer relationships as a benefit.
- Focus on wellness and wholeness.
- Emphasize the service you will provide as their Upline.
- Make it easy and simple to do.
- They may not ask for information because they are concerned about pleasing you more than getting their own needs met. Be sure to help them feel comfortable in getting all their questions answered.
- Tell them how your follow through will be designed for their personal situation.
- Show how much you care about them.
- Give them a guarantee.

After the Registration

- Give them consistent, hands-on follow through.
- Give them a simple way to communicate with you about their progress, so they know you are involved in what they are doing.
- Show them specific steps to take the products or build the business.
- Maintain a friendship by calling regularly and having quality time.

Professors

- Task-Oriented
- Inward
- Rationale Driven
- Strategic Leaders

Professors are often lower key and more soft spoken than any other type. They are typically efficient, curious, experimental, non-dogmatic, complex, impersonal, and independent. They try their best to be accurate, to get things straight, and to sort things out.

Many Professors can be very articulate but may not be sensitive to signals that the listener has had enough and that they need to listen, too. They will tend to talk past a listener's receptivity threshold.

Problem solving is a 24-hour occupation for a Professor. If they don't have a problem, they will find one to exercise their skills in developing models, maps, and paradigms. Although they aren't very 'touchy-feely', they deeply care. They experience being cared about by being asked to talk about their opinion and then listened to.

Because Professors are so focused on being exact and understanding precisely, you will see them correct others' language, ask questions to ensure clarity and attempt to eliminate any ambiguity in a conversation.

Although Professors are Inward, their sense of intuitively understanding the emotional cues given off by others is limited. Rather, they are particularly sensitive to the world of thoughts, ideas, and concepts.

Professors are critical, by nature. Because they are constantly evaluating data for accuracy, any inconsistency is painful, so they will point out errors and any incorrect information.

Why You Need a Professor on Your Team

Professors are excellent strategists because they love to analyze situations and data. You will increase the likelihood of achieving success in your Network Marketing enterprise by having a system to follow and Professors create systems. You need a good Professor on your team to evaluate the costs vs. benefits and set a course for everyone to follow, and to set an alternate course if one particular strategy isn't working.

How to Recognize a Professor

Word Usage

- *Let's look at this logically*
- *What are the guidelines?*
- *What do you mean?*
- Talks about data and features
- Will qualify statements with words like probably, usually, likely, etc.
- May use highly technical terms
- Will notice when others use words incorrectly and correct them
- Language is filled with possibilities, postulates, premises hypotheses, and theorems
- Prefers theories and abstractions and likes to have data and facts to validate them

Vocal

- Uses the least inflection of any type
- They enunciate their words clearly
- Sounds neutral and objective

Visual

- Few facial expressions
- Not inclined toward touching

Key Qualities

- Dependable, detailed, factual
- Careful and cautious
- Sees the glass as half empty
- Desires order, accuracy, perfection
- Wants 'just the facts'
- Has trouble making decisions because they 'don't have all the facts', so procrastinates
- Prefers tasks over people
- Patient, cautious and thorough
- Wants clearly defined priorities and pace
- Willing to do the task alone
- Will share information only on a 'need to know' basis
- Hard to be persuaded otherwise once a decision is made. Loyal to their team and company

What Drives a Professor

Professors need to know and understand. They love to accumulate more and more useful knowledge, rarely deleting or forgetting any, and to work continuously on solutions to the many problems that intrigue them.

They want gratitude from others and want to be praised for being thorough. Professors like it when you ask them questions to show you how much they know.

How Professors Build the Business

- They take the business very seriously, expecting to be judged by their attention to detail.
- Laboriously, they plan a great complicated, complete and accurate system, including all the science and compensation information.
- They figure out how each team member can build the business on his or her own, in case they can't be there for them.
- They build the business largely by themselves and become the 'expert' that everyone relies on for detailed, accurate information.
- They don't expect building the business to be fun, but like to think that their work might result in a significant milestone.

Here is an example of how a Professor would talk to a prospect in a sampling program:

"I would like to make an appointment with you to get your feedback and provide you with documentation and more information. Is next Tuesday at 2 good for you? "

Here, you will notice that Professors want to ensure that the prospect receives relevant, detailed information so they can make an informed decision, whereas the Angel will simply ask how the prospect is feeling when doing the follow up. The underlying intention below the Professor's language is, *"What else do you need to know before you make a sound decision?"*

The Four Subtypes of Professors

Thinking Professor

- Focuses on possibilities
- Has a great need for privacy
- Not influenced by titles or rank
- Values precision, order and accuracy
- Avoids volatile or overly direct people

Directing Professor

- Quiet and serious
- Dependable and keeps their word
- Future focused
- Decisive

Influencing Professor

- Has a strong drive to help others
- Relates well to people but prefers a private lifestyle with few friends
- Highly aware of other people's emotions
- Associates self worth with work
- Not attentive to details

Relating Professor

- Most inward acting of all styles
- Diplomatic and accommodating
- Always sees both better and worse ways to do things so can become confused.
- Dislikes opposition and adversity

Recruiting a Professor

- Prove in writing the quality and value of your product and yourself as a leader.
- Do not rush them.
- Do not embellish or over sell.
- Tell them what you *think*, not what you *feel*.
- Be prepared for them to comparison shop by emphasizing your product or opportunity's strengths.
- Give them time to study the options.
- Help them make a commitment by asking, "What else do you need to know before you make a decision?"

After the Registration

- In your follow up information, be sure to provide education on how they can track their own progress and training.
- Ask them how they would like you to stay in touch with them, how often, and for how long.
- Focus on what the product or opportunity has accomplished and how well it has done so.
- Demonstrate cases where the product or opportunity has worked for others.
- Give them as much detailed educational material as they want. They can never know too much.

Who Do You Know?

Who do I know that is a Professor?

_____

Who do I know that is an Angel?

_____

Who do I know that is a Captain?

_____

Who do I know that is an Entertainer?

_____

Think about the people in your life: who you have easily gotten along with and who have been challenges for you. What kinds of people would you like to have in your organization who are not already there? How are you going to attract them?

Start applying the tools on the Cheat Sheet and practice communicating with different people, so you can have a more successful and fulfilling business.

Further, if you want to develop your skills in a group setting, contact me to do a day-long workshop in your area. We have found that role-playing and interaction in a safe setting are the best ways to learn these skills.

The History of Quadrant Personality Typing

It all started in 370 BC with Hippocrates. He was a physician who was the first person to divide people into one of four types that he called *humors*, based on which system in the body he thought predominated in a person: The Sanguine, The Phlegmatic, The Melancholic, and The Choleric.

Plato (340 BC) was interested in people's contribution to social order, so adapted Hippocrates' theory and divided people into four types based on a social order scale. His pupil, Aristotle (325 BC) defined people on the basis of how they look for happiness, which he called Hedonistic, Proprietary, Ethical, and Dialectical.

Almost 500 years later, the physician Galen (190 AD) developed the terms of Hippocrates and applied them to actual personality. I think that is why his terms endured more than any others did over the years. He was the first person to promote the idea that physiology, not determines temperament. Another 1350 years passed before Paracelsus (1550) added his own thoughts to quadrant typology, incorporating animal names to describe personality types.

In the latter half of the 1800's, science began to predominate and the field of psychology changed from the study of the mind to the study of behavior, introducing the nature or nurture debate. State theory -- the belief that 'who we are' is determined solely by the environment -- emerged as a determinant of behavior for the first time. The father of modern psychology, Wilhelm Wundt, initiated the belief that the brain, rather than the spirit is responsible for personality, leading the way for the development of psychiatry.

The main contributor to trait theory at the time was Ivan Pavlov who, around the turn of the century, theorized that we function solely through stimulus response mechanisms – or instincts – as are other mammals, and are programmed to react. Freud, too, believed that we are mere animals and have no free will or self-determinism.

In the midst of this paradigm in thinking about being a human being versus being a human animal, Carl Jung appeared. He was originally a peer of Freud's but parted ways and initiated a revival in quadrant personality typing, along with the idea that we are more spirit than animal. In the 1920's he worked out a complex personality theory based on extraversion versus introversion combined with preference for one of four basic psychological functions: Thinking, Feeling, Sensation, and Intuition.

In 1958, Isabel Myers and Kathryn Briggs created a test based on the work of Carl Jung that identified sixteen basic personality types, which became a favorite method for identifying career interests in universities.

After that, the Marsden DISC was developed. This was a tool used in business to identify personality types so human resources personnel could correctly assign people to tasks in terms of their social orientation: Driver (Red), Entertainer (Blue), Steady (Green), and Compliant (Yellow).

The most current personality theorists familiar to Network Marketers are Tony Allesandra and Dani Johnson. Tony Allesandra developed his 'People IQ" training in the early 1990's.

Dani Johnson, who became well known in the first decade of the 21st century, re-named the types based on precious stones.

Chart of Quadrant Theorists
and Their Types

Theorist	Type 1	Type 2	Type 3	Type 4
Hippocrates 380 BC	Blood	Yellow Bile	Black Bile	Phlegm
Plato 340 BC	Iconic Artisan	Pistic Caretaker	Dianoetic Researcher	Noetic Moral
Aristotle 325 BC	Hedonistic	Proprietary	Dialectical	Ethical
Galen 190	Sanguine	Choleric	Melancholic	Phlegmatic
Paracelsus 1550	Salamanders Impulsive	Gnomes Industrious	Nymphs Inspired	Sylphs Calm
Marston DISC 1921	**Influencer** Blue	Driver Red	Steady Green	Conservative Yellow
Myers/Briggs 1958 Based on Jung 1923	Extraverted/ Perceptual (EP)	Extraverted/ Judgmental (EJ)	Introverted/ Thinking (IT)	Introverted/ Feeling (IF)
Tony Allesandra 1984	Socializer	**Director**	**Thinker**	**Relater**
Dani Johnson 2005	Sapphire	Ruby	Emerald	Pearl

Resources

Mastery: The keys to success and long-term fulfillment, by George Leonard

Now, Discover your Strengths by Marcus Buckingham and Donald O. Clifton

The Platinum Rule by Tony Allesandra
http://www.alessandra.com

Please Understand Me by David Keirsey and Marilyn Bates

Please Understand Me II by David Keirsey

Personality Plus by Florence Littauer

Personality Puzzle by Florence Littauer and Marita Littauer

Relationship Strategies by Dr. Tony Allesandra. Six CD set. This is the most useful study of the types I have found. There are numerous examples of what people say, how they sound, how to help them in the sales process, and how to relate to them.
http://www.alessandra.com

Revolutionary Agreements, by Marian Head
www.revolutionaryagreements.com

Recruiting/Retention Cheat Sheet

Captain	Entertainer
Behaviors	
Steady eye contact	Steady eye contact
Seems impatient	Inflection in speech
Poor at small talk	Tells stories and jokes
Emphatic language	Lots of hand gestures
Firm handshake	Spontaneous touching
Recruiting	
Let them control the process	Tell them stories about people
Provide all the pertinent info the first time.	Show how we provide status, recognition and excitement
Don't give lots of details	Be enthusiastic
Use thinking words	Use feeling words
Get to the bottom line	Talk faster
Show how to gain power	No details – fun and easy
Do you want to join our business? Yes or No.	*Where do we go from here?*
Retention	
Send follow up information showing your commitment to their getting results.	Help with the details. Do it for them because they don't read the directions.
Ask them how you are doing with them.	Remind them they made the right choice
Provide a self-directed training system to do on their own	Show them how to use the products.
Talk business, not relationship.	Have regular contact in social situations that are fun and upbeat.

Recruiting/Retention Cheat Sheet

Angel	Professor
Behaviors	
One-on-one eye contact	Poor eye contact
Speaks slowly and calmly	Enunciates words
Good listener	Doesn't like touching
Talks about feelings	Uses analytical language
Warm handshake	Light handshake
Recruiting	
Show them you care about them	Written validation on you, product, and business
Mention names of people they know	Do not over sell
Use feeling words	Use thinking words
Focus on contribution and wholeness	Focus on details, rationale, features.
Easy and simple	Do not over sell
Provide gentle nudges to get to commitment	Make follow up calls to answer their questions
Encourage their questions so they don't regret their decision	*What else do you need to know before making your decision?*
Retention	
Provide consistent, hands-on training	Provide a system for tracking their progress
Provide simple communication methods	Ask them how you should support them
Show them specific steps to build the business	Focus on the results of the products and business
Maintain a friendship by having quality time with them.	Show how the product and business has worked for others